בס"ד

לד' הארץ ומלואה

THIS BOOK BELONGS TO:

_____

Please read it to me!

A Chanuka & Purim Journey

© 2024

All rights reserved to the author and illustrator,
Menachem Mendel Gershon

First edition – Kislev 5785

For orders and other inquiries:
info.mmbooks@gmail.com

Visit our website for various ordering options,
free fun pages, and more!

TheMMbooks.com

Your Journey Highlights

Victory of the Maccabees 1

Oil Jug Miraculously Found 2

Spinning the Dreidel 3

Lighting the Menorah 4

Giving Chanuka Gelt 5

Sizzling Latkes 6

Oily Donuts 7

Outnumbering the Darkness 8

Lighting Up the World 9

Tidbits of the Chanuka Story 10

Tidbits of the Purim Story 11

Listening to the Megilah 12

Giving Mishloach Manos 13

Gifts to the Poor 14

The Purim Feast 15

Dressing Up 16

Tasty Hamantashen 17

Evil Haman 18

Mordechai & Esther Celebrate 19

Simcha for the Entire Year...........................20

The Maccabees took their weapons to fight
victory was theirs, what a great sight
Few against many, they miraculously won
that's why we celebrate and have so much fun

The Beis Hamikdash was such a mess
one oil jug was discovered, what a Nes!
Making more oil would arrive too late
instead, it lasted for eight nights straight

On Chanuka, the Dreidel we play and spin
it has the letters Nun, Gimmel, Hei, and Shin
Nun stands for 'miracle,' and Gimmel for 'great'
Hei for 'happened,' and Shin, 'there' He did create

Now it's already night number two
everyone's shouting Yahoo!
We got the hang of the Chanuka lights
I see a donut, I'll go take a few bites

We have a tradition of giving Chanuka Gelt
not made of chocolate, that kind could melt

It's part of Chinuch — the child's education
to give some to Tzedaka, for the Jewish nation

A special food we eat on this day
potato pancakes called "Latkes," hurray!
Take it from the pan when it's sizzling hot,
there's plenty for all, so take a lot!

I eat a donut, it's really yummy
after a few bites, it's all in my tummy
Like the Latkes, it has oil galore
oil for the Menorah was found in the floor

Now it's already night number five
this night is extra special so let's take a dive
We're lighting five candles tonight
darkness is outnumbered by light

The Menorah can be made of silver or gold
candles numbering the night we hold
The world is lit up from the Menorah's light
and against all the darkness we will fight

I'm Mr. Dreidel, and I want to tell you a bit about Chanuka. A long, long time ago, the Greeks wanted Jews to behave like them. They even made golden altars in the city squares to sacrifice treif animals.

Chana had seven sons. Antiochos tried to make them bow down, but they refused, and he killed them.

Matisyahu's five sons—Eliezer, Yehudah, Shimon, Yochanan, and Yonasan—led the Maccabees who fought the Greeks, and they always won. During one of the battles, Eliezer got killed by an elephant.

The Jews hid in caves to learn Torah, and when the Greek soldiers came, they started playing with me—I remember it like yesterday.

When they returned to the Beis Hamikdash, it was a big mess. There wasn't any pure oil to light the Menorah, because the Greeks broke all the jugs. Finally, they found one jug of oil for one day, but it would take eight days until they could get more oil.

Hashem made a miracle and it lasted for eight days. That's why we light a Menorah for eight days and eat oily foods like Latkes and donuts. Have a HAPPY CHANUKA, and enjoy spinning me!

I'm Mr. Hamantash, and I would like to share some of the Purim story: A long time ago, King Achashverosh made a great feast and invited all of Shushan to come. They served almost everything—that's except for me. He even invited the Jews, but this was a big problem because it had non-kosher food. Mordechai told the Jews not to go, but some Jews didn't listen.

At the party, Achashverosh got very drunk, and when his queen disobeyed him, he had her killed. Later, he wanted a new queen, so he gathered girls from all over his kingdom. Esther tried to hide, but she was found, and she was chosen. At Mordechai's request, she didn't reveal her Jewishness.

Achashverosh had an evil minister named Haman, who hated the Jews. He wanted to destroy them, so he got Achashverosh to sign a decree to kill all Jews on the 13th of Adar.

Mordechai gathered all the children and Davened with them. He also sent a message to Esther to do something about it, so Esther said that all the Jews should fast for three days and nights, and then she'll go to the king.

When she came, the King asked what she wanted, and she asked that he and Haman come to a party. At the second party, Esther finally told Achashverosh that Haman wanted to kill her very own nation, and then Haman was hanged.

That's why we make a great celebration, and please put me on your invitation. Have a HAPPY PURIM!!!

The Megilah is made from parchment and ink
when we read it, about the story we think
By night and by day, it's read out loud
for one person, or even better, a crowd

We give Mishloach Manos to another
a friend, a cousin, or maybe your brother
Two kinds of foods, but they can be one Bracha
that's how it works according to Halacha

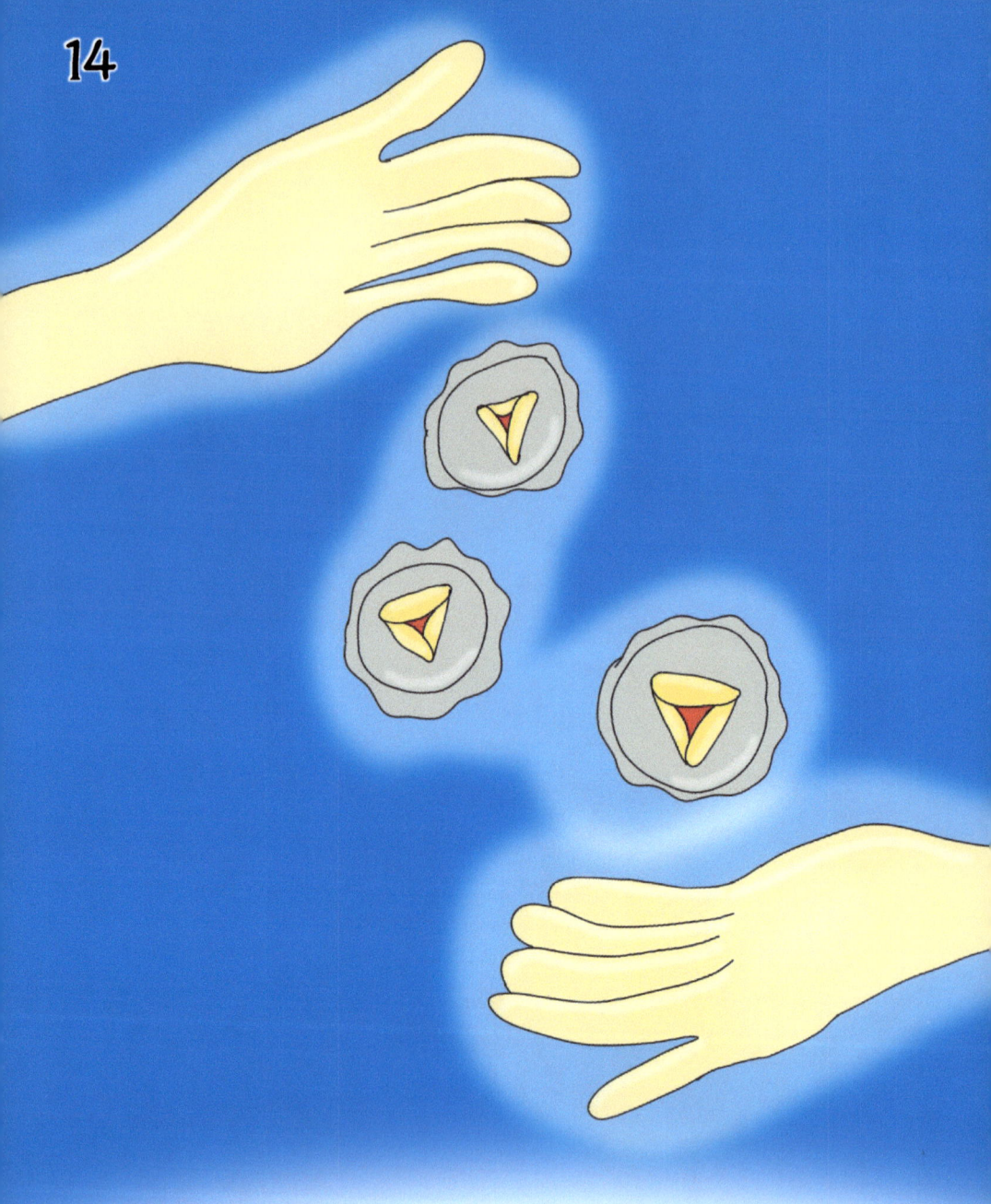

We give some money to the poor
anyone who might knock on the door
People might ask you for money a lot
so on Purim, carry money in every spot

We eat a meal that's very delicious
a Purim feast that may be nutritious
Challah, fish, meat, and wine
With Simcha, let's celebrate and dine

On Purim, costumes we love to see
every single one, like a truck or a tree
And maybe a clown, a robot, or honey
a toy, or a book, it's always funny

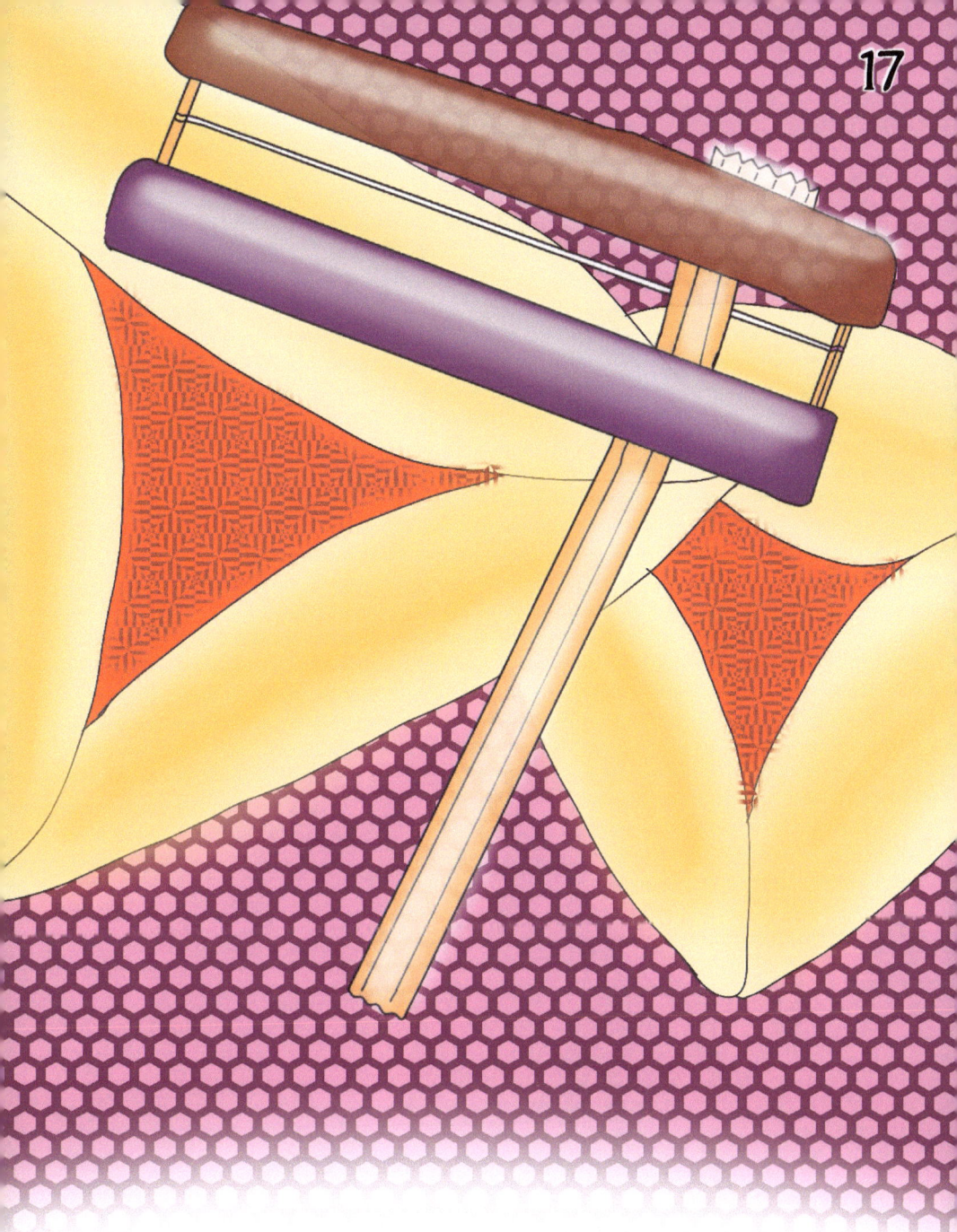

On Purim we eat a kind of nosh,
a triangular cookie called a Hamantash
With Graggers we make a lot of noise,
let's hear it, all you girls and boys!

Haman was very bad, evil, notorious
he had a plan, but the Jews were victorious
Hashem protected the Jews, that's us!
Haman was killed 'cause he made such a fuss

Haman's servants reported, they sure didn't lie
he was hanged on his own gallows, so high

He tried to kill Queen Esther's nation
instead, he was killed—what a celebration!

Nissan is coming, Adar is done
boy, that was a lot of fun!
Purim by far is the happiest day
pack up the joy so it will stay

THE END

Thanks for reading!

Hope you enjoyed your journey, and see you back again next year!

Download free fun pages at TheMMbooks.com

- Coloring sheets
- Color-by-number
- Dot-to-dot
- Draw step-by-step
- And more!

The Yom Tov Journeys Series

Collect them all!

www.ingramcontent.com/pod-product-compliance
Lightning Source LLC
LaVergne TN
LVHW070048070526
838201LV00036B/361